51 COMMON BRANDING AND MARKETING MISTAKES AND HOW TO FIX THEM

Ires D. Alliston

PRAISES

"I know Ires for 5 years and during this time she have had answer any questions that I had with open arms and no hesitation. I had the wonderful opportunity to talk with Ires today. I learned a wealth of information from her that I will now use for to build my brand and my Send Out Cards business. I am so very excited to incorporate the many tools she has had shared." – *Nadia Torabi, Entrepreneur*

"Wonderful experience!!! I reached out to Ires and within moments I received a reply as well as a prompt time to converse that day! We spoke and got right to business on how to start building my brand onto a website, which was exactly what i asked for. Her professionalism poured right through as soon as we spoke of my ideas and vision! I am excited and pleased to have her be a part of my business journey! Thank you partner!" – *Chantell Thompson, Speaker, Trainer & Coach*

"5 Stars!!!!! I had the wonderful opportunity to talk with Ires today. I learned a wealth of information from her that I will now use for to build my brand and business. I am so very excited to incorporate the many tools she shared. I am more excited to continue to work with Ires, as this is only the beginning! I highly recommend everyone who wants to grow their business to take advantage of the extraordinary wisdom she offers!" – *Julie Duncan, Entrepreneur*

"Ires truly has a heart for helping others succeed. She is an amazing business woman and it has been such a pleasure to have met her. If you are looking to taking your business to another level, Ires is truly the business women you want to work with. Ires is and always will be a Blessing to others!" – *Fran Hurley, Entrepreneur*

"Thanks to the BEST Branding and Marketing Coach! I've learned so much from Ires. There's a difference between branding and marketing. I highly recommend Ires as a branding coach. I want to thank you so very much. You rock! You are the best! – *Betty Riddick, Mind, Body, and Soul Expert and International Speaker*

"Ires is an awesome person! We were talking on the phone for 20 minutes and she went into branding and marketing mode and gave me this plan. And I said, "that's a WOW, girl!" What can I do to be your

client?" If you need a branding and marketing expert, you need to go to Ires. She is the beast and I endorse her!" – ***Dr. Ira Roach III, International Speaker, Trainer and Coach***

Ires D. Alliston

Copyright © 2018 by Ires D. Alliston

Cover and Internal Design by Ires D. Alliston

Published by The Alliston Group, LLC

ALL RIGHTS RESERVED. No part of this book may be reproduced in any form or by any electronic or mechanical means including information storage, retrieval systems, photocopying, recording or otherwise – except in the case of brief quotations embodied in articles or reviews – without permission in writing from its publisher, The Alliston Group, LLC.

All brand names and product used in this book are trademarks, registered, or trade names of their respective holders.

ACKNOWLEDGEMENT

Once again, I'm forever grateful to the following people in my life and God –

My family – my husband, Duane, my two sons who are now young men, Michael and Matthew (my M&M kids), I'm blessed to have you in my life! You continue to inspire and believe in me to no end.

My business partner and confidant, Jacqueline T. Hill for bringing her heart, and vision to the forefront so I may see it clearer and easier.

To my beloved family, I carry you with me, always. You're always in my heart, mind and prayers. Your spirit is everlasting.

I'm eternally grateful to God. I trust in you. You have plans for me and my family – beyond words and sight. Please continue to bless me with the knowledge, skills, strengths, courage and compassion to serve others.

Last but not least, special thanks…

To my clients, students and friends who make it all possible. You inspire me endlessly.

And to you, awesome reader, for making this purchase, for your valuable time and attention.

Table of Contents

ACKNOWLEDGEMENT v
Introduction... 1
What is Branding? 2
What is Marketing? 4
    Branding is Strategic While Marketing is Tactical 5
    Branding Makes Loyal Customers While Marketing Activates Buyers..... 5
51 Common Branding and Marketing Mistakes and How to Fix Them........ 6
1. Not Thinking About How Your Brand Will be Received 7
2. Inconsistency Across Different platform................................... 9
3. Relying Too Much on Design Trend... 11
4. Attaching Your Brand to Wrong Things................................... 12
5. Deviating from What Made Your Brand Successful in the First Place..... 14
6. Using Copy That Doesn't Describe Your Brand Accurately 15
7. Not Measuring Your Brand Activities 16
8. No Honesty... 17
9. Choosing the Wrong Niche to Brand Yourself in..................... 18
10. Being too Lazy 19
11. Having too Many Social Profiles 20
12. Screaming Your Sales Pitch 21
13. Your Product is Not Meeting People's Need......................... 22
14. Botching Your Email Personalization Tags 23

15. Not Making Essential Form Fields Required 24
16. Sending Email to the Wrong List 25
17. Using Out-dated, Bad or Not Credible Data 26
18. Publishing Your Content Prematurely 27
19. Not Double Checking the Time and Date to Publish Your Content....... 28
20. No Unsubscribe Option in Your Email 29
21. Not Including CTAs (Call-to-Action) in Your Blog Post 30
22. Not Configuring Links to Open in Another Window 31
23. Not Having a Website... 32
24. Not Making Your Website Mobile Friendly 33
25. Adding Distraction to Your Landing Page... 34
26. Not Linking to Your Website in Your Social Media Updates and Profiles 35
27. Overlooking Formatting and Images in Your Blog Posts 36
28. The Absence of a Download Link on Email and Thank You Pages 37
29. Linking Your Call to Action to a Wrong Landing Page 38
30. Not Writing Meta Description 39
31. Marketing the Same Product to People Who Have Bought it 40
32. Not Checking Your Broken Links and Cleaning up Dead Pages 41
33. Buying or Renting Email List... 42
34. Not Adding Share Button or Follow Button in Your Content 43
35. Not Giving Your Audience a Means of Contacting You 44
36. Ignoring SEO 45
37. Not Blogging 46
38. Not Getting Local Search 47

vii

39. Not Using Social Media 48
40. Misusing Happy Customers 49
41. Not Speaking at Conferences 50
42. Neglecting Affiliate 51
43. Failure to Network 52
44. Not Commenting on Blogs 53
45. Not Accepting Referrals 54
46. Not Using Video Marketing 55
47. Not Offering Special Deals 56
48. Poor Customer Service 57
49. Too Lazy about Getting Press 58
50. Poor Network Management 59
51. Poor Brand Management 60
Get your Branding and Marketing on the Right Track 61
Ires Alliston' Famous Quotes: 62
About Ires Alliston - 71
Media Contact – 72
Bonus 1: 73
Bonus 2: 74

Introduction

When it comes to branding and marketing, business owners often confuse branding for marketing. In fact, many marketing agencies, organizations let alone marketing departments make the common mistake. Which is why many businesses make similar branding and marketing mistakes as well.

It is not new that many business owners struggle in building and marketing their brand properly. If you get your strategy wrong from the start, in other words, if the foundation is not created properly, you may find it difficult to build a strong brand.

Let's set the record straight; branding is not marketing, and marketing is not branding! Before we start analyzing the branding and marketing mistakes and how to fix them, first, let's get familiar with the real meaning of marketing and branding.

What is Branding?

Photo Credit: Peggy Marco Lachmann

Branding is what your business stands for. We can also say that branding is promise delivered! It is true that branding has to do with your brand's badge, logo, website, name and color but those are just the tiny fractions of the real meaning of branding. Branding is the promise you make to your customers and how you deliver your promise.

To define your brand, you need to identify your target audience, what they want, help them create their unique selling proposition that sets them apart from competitors, and craft a statement that explains their brand's purpose.

Defining what your brand stands for will make it easier for you to make decisions. For instance, what product to sell, who to hire, what your office will look like and how to communicate with your audience.

If you have a company or organization, to unlock your brand's power, you need to involve your employees. Let them understand the process and make sure you have a brand expert to help guide you. Getting a brand expert to guide you and can assist you in setting a brand strategy can eliminate a lot of the guesswork in building the foundation of your brand.

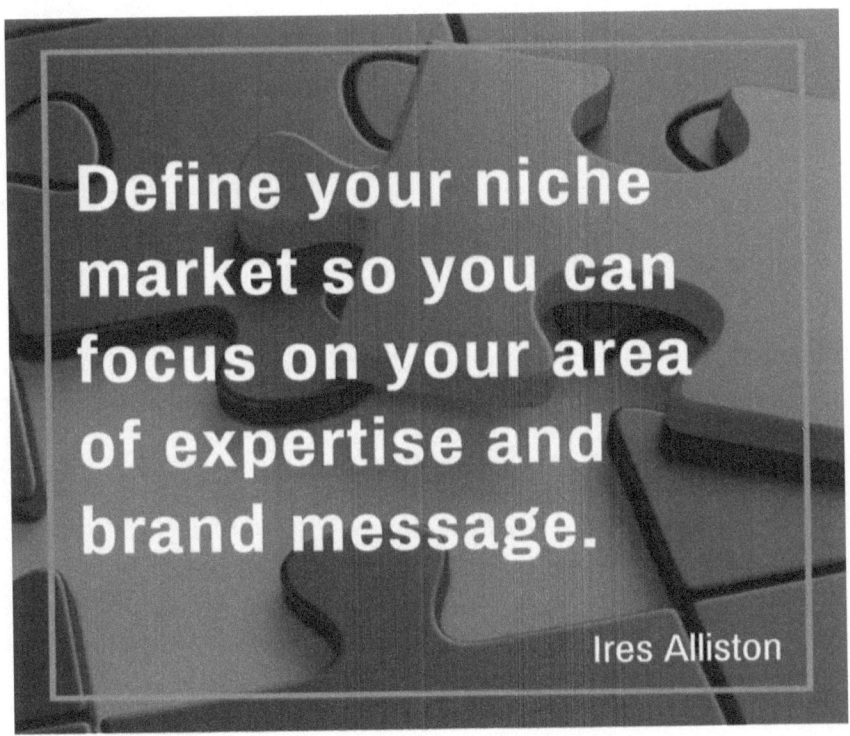

What is Marketing?

Photo Credit: Darwin Laganzon

Marketing is identifying what consumers want and creating a solution to their problem that meets their needs. By developing the product or service that offers value and promoting it to the audience, you are bringing awareness of the product's existence in the marketplace.

After creating your brand, marketing becomes an integral part of it because it is the marketing that will help you communicate your promise to your audience

In short, marketing is everything you do to get your promise or message to customers, while branding is how you keep your promise through delivery to your customer. Marketing may contribute to your brand, but your brand is bigger than all your marketing effort. If you get your branding wrong, and/or do not establish as strong brand foundation, your marketing effort may be fruitless.

Branding is Strategic While Marketing is Tactical

After marketing has swept through the room, it is only the brand that will remain. The brand is what sticks in the mind in association with the company, organization, product or service – whether one buys at the moment or not.

The brand also determines whether customers will be loyal or not. Marketing may push you to buy an Audi, but the brand will determine if you will only buy an Audi for the rest of your life. You can build your brand on many things but the most important among them is the experience you give and offer to consumers – which is part of the brand. Did the Honda deliver on the brand promise of reliability? Did the maker continue upholding the quality standards that made them what they are? Did the service center mechanic or sales guy know what they are talking about?

Branding Makes Loyal Customers While Marketing Activates Buyers

Whether profit or non-profit, all organizations must sell. This works the same way for all organizations or businesses. How each organization or business sell may differ, but they are all working to achieve the same thing. Every thought, every ad, every policy, every action and every marketing promotion has the effect of either inspiring or deterring brand loyalty in whoever is exposed to it because all of it affects sales.

Once again, branding is a vital foundation for a successful operation of the business. Getting your branding right is a recipe for a successful marketing campaign and retaining your customers.

51 Common Branding and Marketing Mistakes and How to Fix Them

A lot of business owner make branding and marketing mistakes. These mistakes can be costly and/or spell doom for any business, which is why it's recommended that you establish a good foundation from the start. However, if you've already made the mistakes and are looking for the way to correct them, you are not alone. I'll be sharing some of the common branding and marketing mistakes and how to correct them in this e-book.

Here's a story -

A company called Colgate jumped into frozen food in 1982 by releasing a Colgate-branded frozen line known as Colgate Kitchen Entrees. The company released the frozen food line because the ready-to-eat meal market was viewed as a great space for a company that is already successful. Unfortunately, the company had just one problem: the brand.

Colgate was a brand known for toothpaste, so the introduction of ready-to-eat meal product under the same brand did not sit well with their consumers. The company had spent many years to build the brand as a toothpaste company, so the new product was not consistent with the existing brand image.

That is an example of branding-gone-wrong. Though their frozen entrees might have been delicious, releasing the product under a wrong brand was a major flop. Therefore, you can't afford to get your branding wrong!

Ok. Let's go straight to branding and marketing mistakes you need to avoid and if you've already fallen to some of them, let alone know what they are, how do you fix them?

1.

Not Thinking About How Your Brand Will be Received

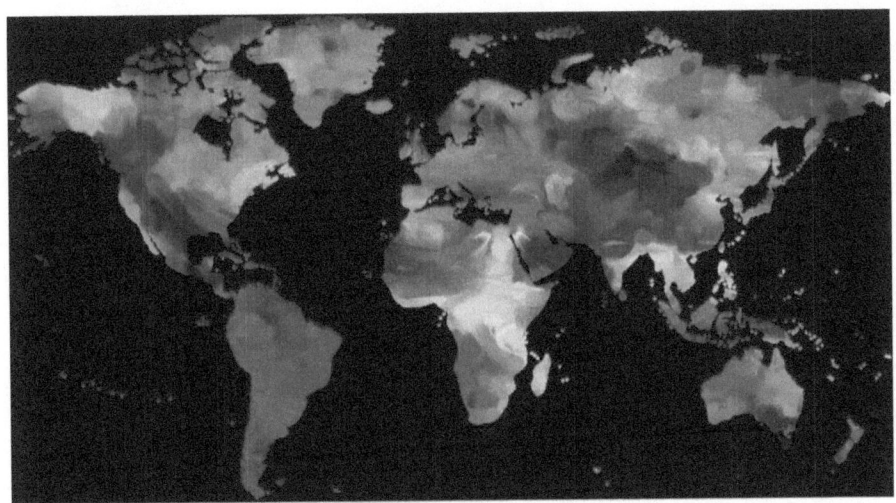

Photo Credit: Schweiz

After determining your audience, the next thing to do is to craft your brand's message. When you are crafting your brand's message, it is important to consider how it might be perceived globally. Even if you are a local business, you never know when people from other parts of the world will show interest in your brand and product. To combat this, you need to create a message that would make scaling your brand globally easy.

One infamous example of a global branding gone wrong was that of Pepsi when it was launched in China with the same American slogan, "Pepsi brings you back to life." To the Chinese, the slogan means "Pepsi brings your ancestors back from the grave." As you may imagine, this did not sit well with the consumers in China because their ancestors are being revered or are deeply respected.

In other words, you can't use "one-size-fits-all" approach when it comes to global branding. What works in one place might not work in another place. If you think you will take your brand global one day, which I often recommend for many personal and business brands, it is better to prepare for it in advance and prepare to localize your brand's message.

2.

Inconsistency Across Different Platform

Photo Credit: Geralt

Consistency is the first rule when it comes to building a strong brand. If you have not been presenting a consistent identity to your audience, you are shooting yourself in the foot. Consistent identity helps you foster a sense of trust for your consumers and build an easily recognizable image for your business. If you are not consistent, you will end up appearing disjointed or disconnected, unprofessional and untrustworthy.

Being consistent starts from your visual assets across every place where your business is represented. This can include your ads, website, print materials, social media accounts, signature email and so forth. It is highly advisable to represent your company with a unique image, logo, color, and everything concerning branding. In addition to being consistent, stay authentic, relevant/relatable and determined in growing your brand!

3.

Relying Too Much on Design Trend

Photo Credit: Rawpixel

It's good to keep up with the latest trend but losing your core identity in the pursuit of the hottest new thing is not advisable, to say the least. You can represent your business in a fresh, contemporary way but don't lose your core identity in the process.

Although, you can get swept up in something that looks cool at the moment, your business will still need to weather a lot of design wave trends. If you're too committed to the trend in design, you risk losing your identity and making your brand look dated.

The bottom line is not to rely too heavily on design trends because they're supposed to only be a source of inspiration.

4.

Attaching Your Brand to Wrong Things

AllistonGroup.com

When it comes to events, sponsorships and branded products, you need to use your logo and name sparingly and selectively. Whatever you want to attach your brand name with it, should be compatible and reflect your brand's values and voice. If you partner with a brand that is not directly related or match your own message, the customer will feel you are inconsistent and it can make it hard for them to trust you in the process.

In 2009, Disney came under fire because it released Montana-branded cherries. The move looked self-involved to their consumers and the

fans of the children TV show were even surprised. Because there is no real connection between the Hannah Montana brand and cherries, that move from Disney was a clear branding blunder. Therefore, make sure you choose the right brand affiliation.

5.

Deviating from What Made Your Brand Successful in the First Place

Photo Credit: Piro4D

You might love to consider a brand redesign maybe because of design trends. It is important not to deviate too much from what made your brand successful in the first place because you want your existing audience to recognize you after the redesign. Suffice to say, making abrupt changes can turn even your loyal fans against your brand.

Make sure you recognize your business core values and image and always keep your consumers and audience at the forefront of everything you do.

6.

Using Copy That Doesn't Describe Your Brand Accurately

Photo Credit: IresAlliston.com

Most businesses fall victim to too vague, over-the-top copywriting that doesn't paint the accurate picture of their brand. If you want to distinguish your brand from the competition, you can't be using the same buzzwords that others are using. You need that element that will make your brand look unique but don't go over-the-top.

7.

Not Measuring Your Brand Activities

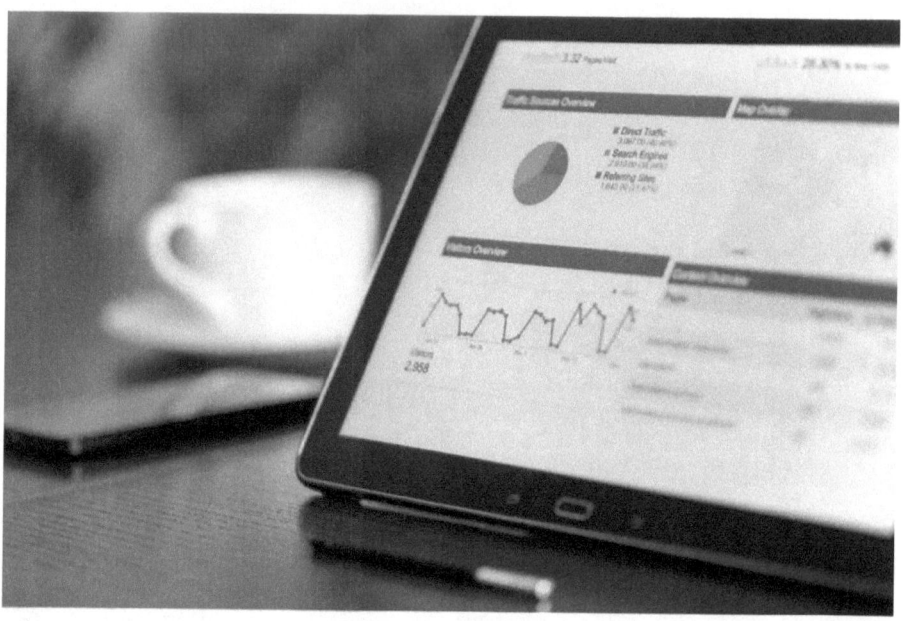

Photo Credit: PhotoMIX-Company

One of the branding problems a lot of businesses face is the inability to track their activities. As a brand, you already have a plan and strategy in place but are you following it? Tracking your activities will help you know what's working and not working for your business. It will also help you catch any areas you may have made mistakes and how to correct them immediately. If you've not been tracking your activities, this is the time to start tracking it so that it can be easy for you to build a strong brand.

8.

No Honesty

Photo Credit: Gerd Altmann

Don't make promises you will not be able to fulfill. Consumers always count on the promise your brand makes. That is why you must make only the promise you're able to keep. Once you disappoint your customers, it may be hard to regain their trust. Or worst, you may not ever again.

It is important to be honest in your dealings and try to deliver on your brand's promise.

9.

Choosing the Wrong Niche to Brand Yourself in

One of the most important decisions in your brand is to make sure you study know your niche and choose the right niche for you. You shouldn't take this approach haphazardly or chances are, you'll get it wrong. Most business owners are branding their companies in a wrong niche, yet they claim they are having a tough time building a strong brand. If you really want to build a strong brand, you need to do it in the right niche.

10.

Being too Lazy

Photo Credit: Wokandapix

Many business owners may copycat other brands or build a general brand. If your brand is not unique or you are just copying another brand, you may find it a challenge for people to trust you and/or your brand. By finding something unique and personalizing it, you will be able to rise above the noise. Once again, instead of just copying someone else entirely, try to find a way to customize it so it'll work for you and your brand.

11.

Having too Many Social Profiles

Photo Credit: Pixaline

Most companies create too many social media profiles than they can manage on a consistent basis. If you can't update your social handle from time to time, your followers will never take you seriously. It is highly advisable that you should create the number of social profiles you can regularly manage or hire a social media manager to update it for you. Again, this goes back to being consistent with your brand.

12.

Screaming Your Sales Pitch

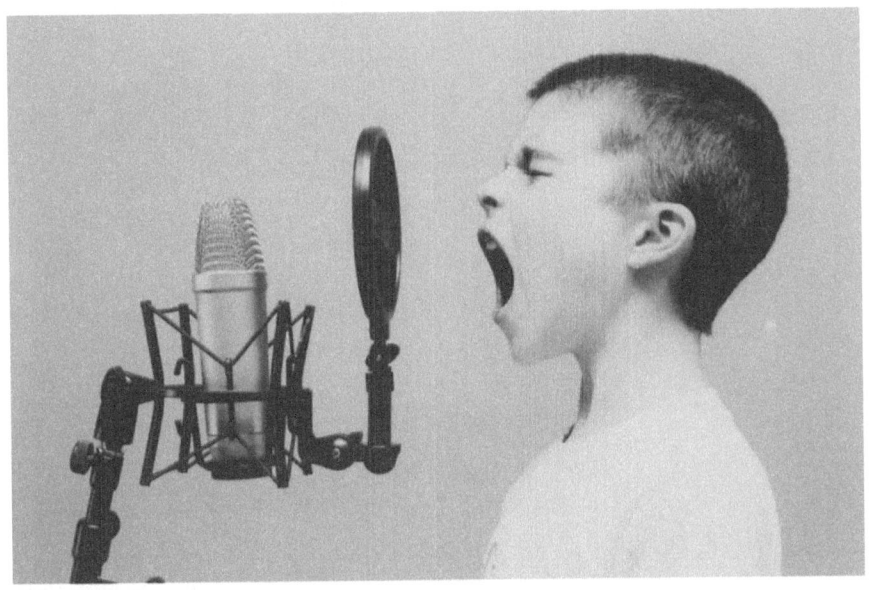

Photo Credit: Free-Photos

One of the biggest marketing mistakes business owners make is spamming every outlet with their sales pitch. Whether you scream your sales pitch or not, the consumer will either like it, not like it or simply ignore it. If you're trying too hard for their attention, it will appear that you're desperate. Make sure you provide valuable and searchable content on the internet that people find useful and beneficial for them.

13.

Your Product is Not Meeting People's Need

Photo Credit: Geralt

The product or service you offer does not matter. The most important thing is how your service or product meets the needs of customers. If you want to market successfully, you need to solve people's problems and alleviate pain. Make sure you demonstrate the benefits of your product or service rather than describing it.

14.

Botching Your Email Personalization Tags

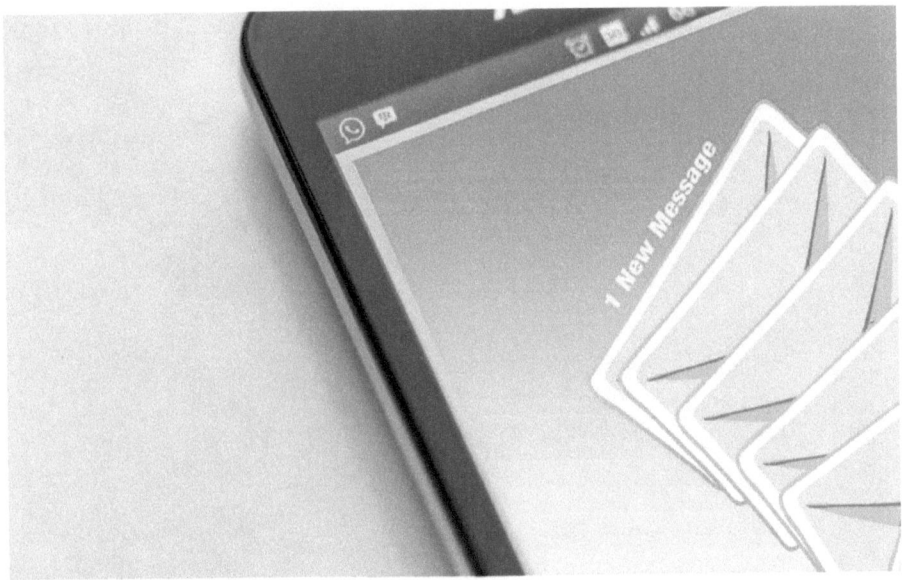

Photo Credit: Geralt

When you are personalizing your tags, or additional information that is attached to a message, make sure you don't mess it up. You can do this by always double checking whether they are correct or not. Also, be sure to set up your default tags in case you don't have information you are personalizing with for a given contact.

15.

Not Making Essential Form Fields Required

Photo Credit: Tero Vesalainen

When you're making the form to capture your website visitors, make sure you asterisk the essential fields like name, email, etc. This will help you to capture the information you need to personalized messages you're sending to your leads. If you're not indicating the compulsory form fields that your website visitors need to fill, you are making a mistake. When you capture the right information, you will be able to personalize your message and provide even more value to your contacts about your product, service or relevant information.

16.

Sending Email to the Wrong List

Photo Credit: Geralt

Are you segmenting your list? In other words, are you creating and dividing your list into smaller groups? If you're not segmenting your list, then you should do it now. This is one of the common mistakes business owners make. Therefore, create groups based on interests, demographics, preferences, just to name a few and don't forget to label them. In doing so, this will help you send your message to the right list. Again, be sure to label your lists clearly and indicate who is on the given list.

17.

Using Out-dated, Bad or Not Credible Data

Photo Credit: Free-Photos

Many companies don't check their data before rolling it out to market their product or service. How would you feel if a person is marketing a product to you using an outdated data? This is a mistake that one should avoid whenever possible. By doing some research online and offline, you can make sure your data is current and accurate.

18.

Publishing Your Content Prematurely

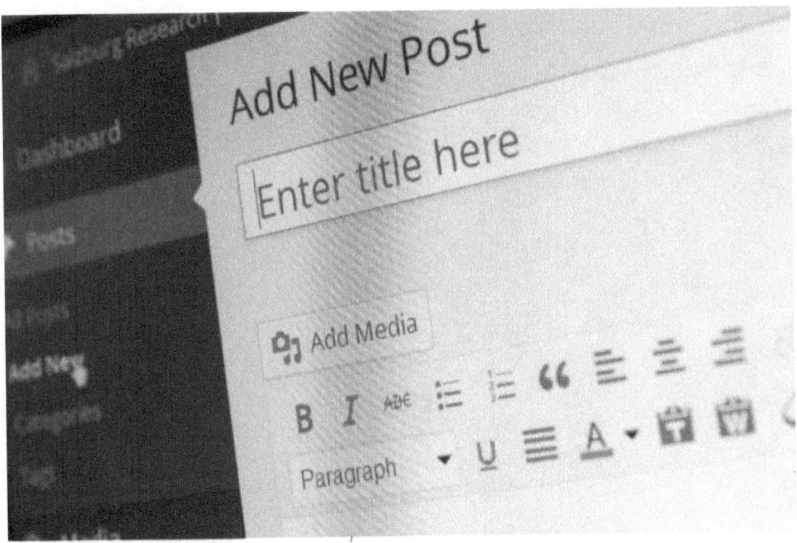

Photo Credit: Pixelcreatures

Most people often fall into this mess and this can happen even to the best of us! Don't be too eager or excited to get your email, landing page or blog post out there without letting more detail-oriented and editorial-minded colleagues give it a look. If you publish content with typos and grammatical errors, it can undermine your credibility and business. It is important that you ask someone who is editorial-minded and more detail-oriented to proof read your content before you get it out there to avoid embarrassing typos and grammatical errors.

19.

Not Double Checking the Time and Date to Publish Your Content

Photo Credit: Congerdesign

If your post is supposed to be scheduled to be published by 6 am for your prospects in Europe but you accidentally schedule it for 6 pm, it means the post will hit the feed of your prospects in the middle of the night when they are sound asleep. If it is a Twitter post, you know the feed has a very short life which can lead to a lost opportunity. So, make sure you double check the time and date so that your content can be received by the right people.

20.

No Unsubscribe Option in Your Email

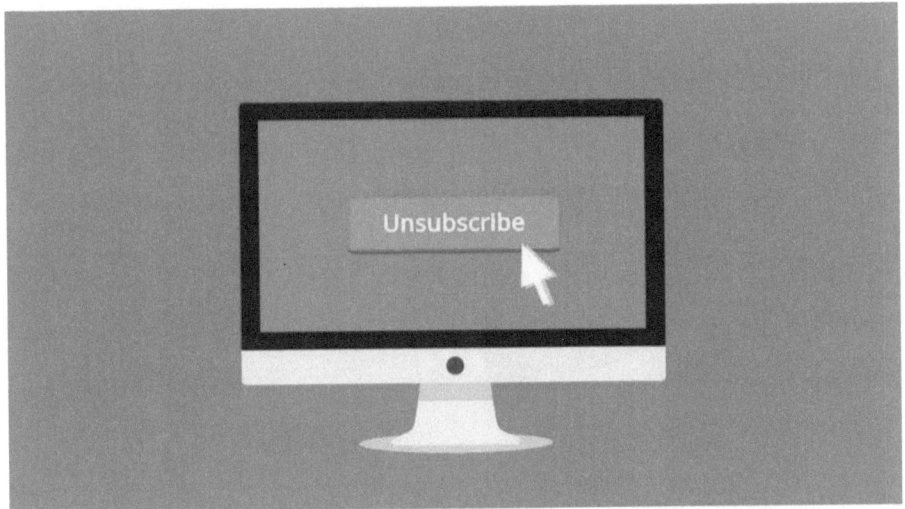

Photo Credit: Bogda13

This is actually illegal because you're not giving people an option here. According to the CAN-SPAM Act, there must be an unsubscribe option to give recipients a chance to unsubscribe from your email list or email campaigns. If email wishes to no longer want to receive your emails, you should make sure you include an unsubscribe option in your email. Thankfully, a lot of email marketing software, if you use them, have this feature already. If you're not using any of them, just double check to have this option included.

21.

Not Including CTAs (Call-to-Action) in Your Blog Post

Photo Credit: Clker-Free-Vector-Images

The gateway to lead generation is a call-to-action. CTAs or call-to-actions are essentially a line of text or image that encourages visitors on your website and customers to act or take action. You should include CTAs in your homepage, every web page, if possible, blog post, landing pages and within your email. If you don't tell them what to do, they will not know the next action to take. However, by stating the action for your prospects to take, it will help them move to the next step.

22.

Not Configuring Links to Open in Another Window

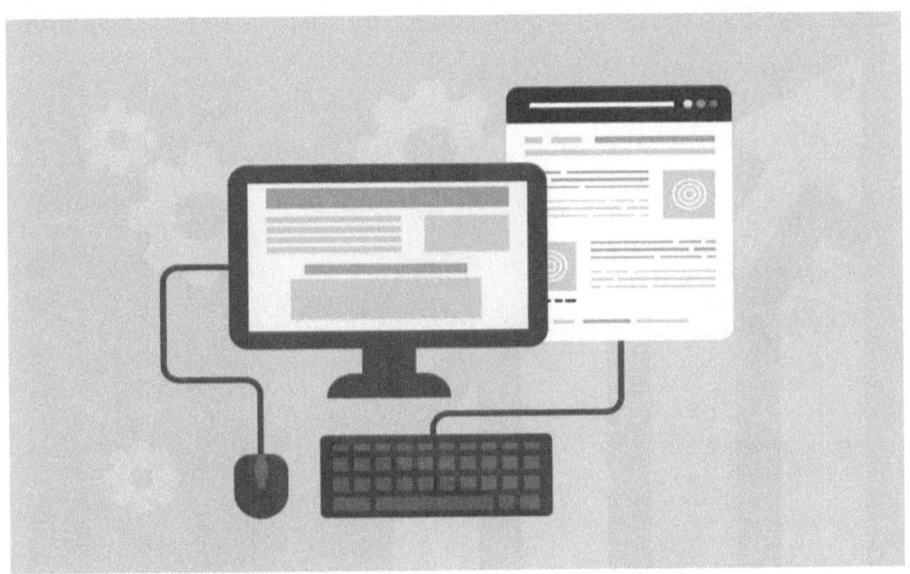

Photo Credit: Kreatikar

If you want your website visitors to stick around for a while, you should configure your links to open in a new window. Imagine having five links on a page and failed to configure those links to open in a new window. It means immediately your website visitor opens the first link, they will be taken to another page and if they don't press the back button, they can't go back to the previous page.

In fact, letting your links open in a new window can help you in your SEO (Search Engine Optimization) because visitors will be able to stay on your website for a longer period and therefore, boost your site's SEO or online ranking.

23.

Not Having a Website

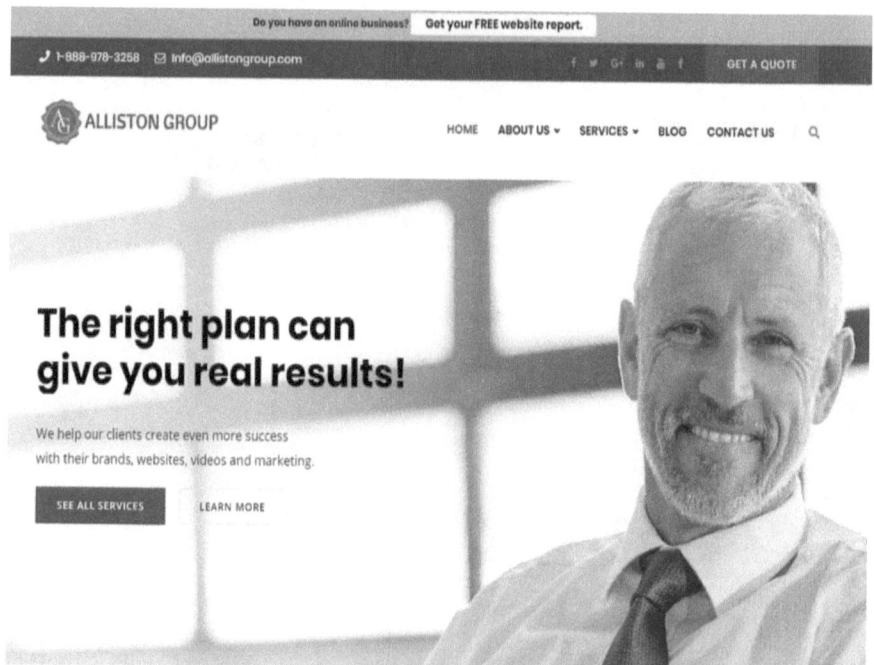

AllistonGroup.com

Almost all businesses are online and if you don't have a website, you are leaving a lot of money on the table. As I often tell my clients and students, your website is your real estate online. It is an online property that you own rather than relying and having your content solely on social media accounts. Therefore, your website should be part of your branding from the start but if you don't have one yet, it is highly recommended that you build one sooner than later! Get a domain name, design a website, and start engaging your audience. If you're not too familiar with all the process, I can certainly help you with this.

24.

Not Making Your Website Mobile Friendly

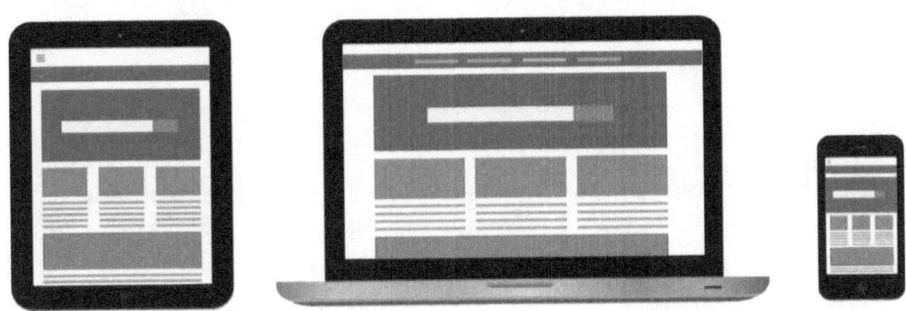

Photo Credit: CoffeeBeanWorks

At least more than 75% of people access websites through their smartphones nowadays. That is why your website needs to be mobile friendly. In fact, Google is now making it compulsory for website owners to make their website mobile friendly. If your website is not mobile friendly, you will lose out in the SEO battle. If your website is outdated or it is not mobile friendly, this is the time to give it a fresh design.

25.

Adding Distraction to Your Landing Page

Photo Credit: JuralMin

Landing pages are standalone web pages that are designed with the main objective. It is to capture people's attention through Call-to-Action. Your landing page is a page you don't want to mess up because it is where you can convert your visitors to leads. Now, if you want to convert your leads to paid customers, you need to remove any distracting elements like side navigation, top navigation and conflicting call to actions, so you can help your visitors to focus on one call to action.

26.

Not Linking to Your Website in Your Social Media Updates and Profiles

Photo Credit: Mike Renpening

When it comes to branding and marketing, your social media profile and updates are important. It is good to have nice content on your social media account but if you're not linking your updates back to your website, you are wasting your effort. Let your audience read your website content too because that is where you can nurture them.

27.

Overlooking Formatting and Images in Your Blog Posts

Photo Credit: Pixel Creatures

After spending hours to write your copy and perfecting it for the next blog post, you need to spice it up. You need visual elements to complement your blog post. You also need to format the post correctly, so the content flows smoothly. Images and formatting are not only good to make website visitors read your blog, they're also good for SEO or Search Engine Optimization. Therefore, make your content shareable by adding images and formatting it properly.

28.

The Absence of a Download Link on Email and Thank You Pages

Photo Credit: Samuel1983

The easiest way to confuse and/or upset your website visitors is to make them go through all the trouble of filling the form with their personal information and not giving them anything in return. The bottom line here is that you need to drop a link for your website visitors to download a free eBook or something after giving you their personal information. Provide even more value and share it!

29.

Linking Your Call to Action to a Wrong Landing Page

Photo Credit: Kobu Agency

This can be devastating when you are sending out an important message to promote an offer. If your link is broken or your CTA leads to a wrong landing page, your visitors will be disappointed. Don't be too eager to get the message out; make sure you double check everything before sending your email to your leads.

30.

Not Writing Meta Description

Photo Credit: FirmBee

Nowadays, people overlook Meta Description (an html tag that summarizes a page's content) because search engines said they were no longer using it. Don't be deceived; solid Meta Description has a place in SEO. You only need less than one minute to write the description! If you don't know how to do this or where to begin, ask the website designer or developer to do this for you.

31.

Marketing the Same Product to People Who Have Bought it

Photo Credit: Trevoy Kelly Photography

This is where defining your website visitor's lifecycle stage comes in. If you can define the lifecycle of your site visitors, it will be easy for you to identify those that have purchased your product and not waste time bothering them again. If your product is so good and they need more of it, they will contact you. So create a list containing the life cycle of your site visitors.

32.

Not Checking Your Broken Links and Cleaning up Dead Pages

Photo Credit: Geralt

Having broken links and pages on your website that are not benefiting your business only makes your site look unprofessional. Not only that, search engines will find it difficult to understand your pages. The bottom line here is to conduct regular audits and clean up dead pages and broken links.

33.

Buying or Renting Email List

Photo Credit: Ribkhan

Why not build your own list? There are several resources to build your list from scratch without much hassle. Renting or buying an email list is a bad idea because you might not be able to personalize the message you will send to them. Some of them will also see your email as spam. It is best to build your own list.

34.

Not Adding Share Button or Follow Button in Your Content

Photo Credit: Monicore

From your blog posts, web page, email to your marketing offer, make sure you include your share button or follow button to make it easy for your recipients or website visitors to share your content with others.

35.

Not Giving Your Audience a Means of Contacting You

Photo Credit: Tumisu

Whether it is your email, phone number or contact form, your website visitors should be able to contact you directly. In case they have questions to ask about your offers or brand, you need to clearly put your contact information on your website, email and social media.

36.

Ignoring SEO

Photo Credit: Simplu27

Small businesses and start-ups are in a good position to leverage Search Engine Optimization, but not many of them know this. With SEO, you can get a higher ranking in search engines and therefore, get a lot of free, targeted traffic on a daily basis. If you're not too familiar with SEO, you can definitely find a lot of information about this topic online.

37.

Not Blogging

Photo Credit: Free Photos

Whatever the type of your business – whether your niche is narrow or huge – you need to start blogging because you will benefit from it. For those who may not be too familiar what a blog is, or what blogging means, it's basically an online journal where you share your content or relevant, valuable topic with your readers. Even Coca-Cola has an active blog – such a big brand. You don't need to buy a separate domain for a blog, you can create a blog section on your company's website. A blog can bring a lot of traffic to your site and help you rank in search engines.

38.

Not Getting Local Search

Photo Credit: JanBaby

For those who may not realize this, search on Google is now hyper-personal. Your search results about a business or businesses online are tailored to your location. So, as a business owner, how do you get local search? Simple. Claim your local search by registering your website on Google My Business. This is especially recommended for brick and mortar businesses.

39.

Not Using Social Media

Photo Credit: Geralt

Some people who don't know much about marketing will think social media is a waste of time. Why even bother! However, look at the statistics of the people that are using social media on a daily basis. This should help determine whether social media is worth it or not for your business. That is where your prospects are, and you need to meet them there.

40.

Misusing Happy Customers

Photo Credit: Geralt

Most companies create happy customers, but they don't leverage their happiness. What you need to do is to contact those happy customers and ask them if you can do a case study for them. Some of them will gladly accept. If you are not doing a case study for them, ask them for testimonials. Testimonials are powerful and can help you attract more customers to your brand. Don't forget to add your testimonials and reviews on your website, marketing flyers and social media platforms. Better yet, ask them to write a review or their thoughts on your social media accounts like under the Facebook review tab, Google review section, Yelp, LinkedIn recommendation area, just to name a few.

41.

Not Speaking at Conferences

Ires Alliston on stage at a Les Brown Summit

If you're one of those business owners who are afraid of speaking at conferences or events in front of a live audience to provide value and be seen as the expert in your niche, you are shooting yourself in the foot. Speaking at conferences can help you build your brand and market your product. Just search for speaking opportunities in your city. In fact, start locally, then go regional, national, and even international. Also, don't just focus on physical locations. You can also try reaching out to experts who can interview you on their podcast, live broadcast, and televised shows. Better yet, you can also do this yourself as well.

42.

Neglecting Affiliate

Photo Credit: Geralt

This is especially good for small businesses and start-ups with a low budget or on shoe-string budget. With a cut in the profit, you can get partners to promote and sell your products. Giving your partners a cut of your profit will motivate them to work more for your company and therefore, help you build your brand even faster.

43.

Failure to Network

Photo Credit: Geralt

Even if you are afraid to speak at conferences, you can at least attend conferences, summits, workshops and social functions. These events will give you a chance to meet new people, build relationships and close business. Although, you might not be able to do business with everyone you meet, you will be able to connect and meet people that can potentially help your business grow.

44.

Not Commenting on Blogs

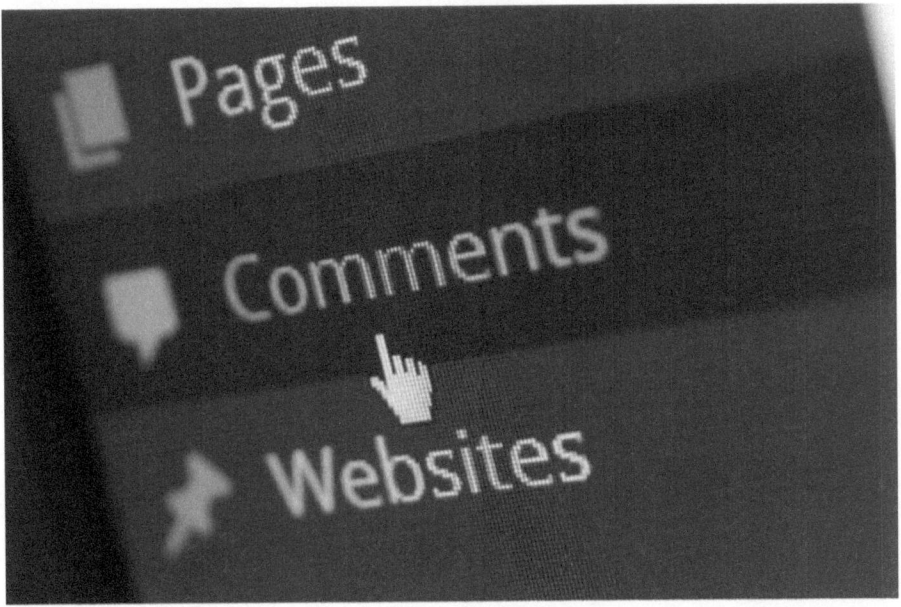

Photo Credit: PixelCreatures

Most people think commenting on blogs is time-consuming and a waste of time. Writing a reasonable comment on blogs related to your niche can help you generate more traffic to your site and help give more exposure to your company. In addition, it can also help build that credible, trustworthy brand because you're providing value to readers and visitors. A word of caution: remember not to spam blog posts!

45.

Not Accepting Referrals

Photo Credit: eConneckt

Many business owners - start-ups, entrepreneurs and companies don't even think to have one in place or create a referral program for their customers and visitors online. Do you know that if you accept the referral, you don't need to spend too much money on marketing? It means all your customers come from a recommendation from satisfied clients. It is simple. You can email them or better yet, call them and ask for referrals after completing a project they love. Chances are they will be happy to refer their followers or someone they know to you who maybe needing your service.

46.

Not Using Video Marketing

YouTube: Ires Alliston

These days, people are not often reading your content online as much as they used to because there are so many contents out there already. However, visual marketing is the next best way to market your brand and products. As you know, when you look at either YouTube or Vimeo, you'll notice the number of people visiting these sites every day is tremendous! You'll understand why videos and video marketing are important. So, start utilizing videos to market your products and services today.

47.

Not Offering Special Deals

Photo Credit: The Digital Artist

Who doesn't like special deals? Although, I don't always recommend to often offer a discount on your products or services as it can reduce your profit margin but imagine the exposure you can get for bringing in a lot of new customers. You can turn those new customers into regular buyers. Find ways to offer special deals for a short time and attract new customers. Also, don't neglect to offer deals to your loyal customers as well. They will appreciate it.

48.

Poor Customer Service

Photo Credit: JeShootscom

Your customer service can make or break your business. We all know that terrible customer service will send customers away. That is why your customer service should be professional and always responds to customer's questions on time.

49.

Too Lazy about Getting Press

Most startups don't always take advantage of how press releases can leverage their brand to that next level. Yet, often, they expect that once they have a website and social media profiles up and running, they expect that exposure and the press to come to them. It doesn't always work this way for a lot us. Although, press agencies and organizations are always looking for news, you should connect or contact them to share your great news, content or article. If they select your article, your content may just get published online!

50.

Poor Network Management

Photo Credit: Rawpixel

Networking is important in business. It is one of the oldest ways to connect and build relationships face to face. But you should network with those that matter. Be strategic with your time by planning and managing your time properly. After all, we all get 86,400 seconds in a day. Question is, how are you going to use every second. Spend quality time with quality people. Manage your network well and manage your time wisely.

51.

Poor Brand Management

Photo Credit: Geralt

If you're not recognizing and correcting at least one of the mistakes listed in this e-book, then you are managing your brand poorly. You need to also see what people are saying about your company (products/services) and find ways to remove negative comments or posts about your company. One great way to manage negative reviews is to address them quickly, try to see it from their point of view and rectify the situation.

Get your Branding and Marketing on the Right Track

Photo Credit: Geralt

It is never too late to get your branding and marketing on the right track. Just make sure you fix all your branding and marketing mistakes and you will see positive results. However, building a solid brand and marketing your product or service is not easy, especially if you have little to no experience to do it. Let alone know where to begin.

My team and I have been helping entrepreneurs and business professionals build credible, trustworthy brands for quite some time now. We can also help you too. If you need any help with your branding and marketing, contact us today.

Ires Alliston' Famous Quotes:

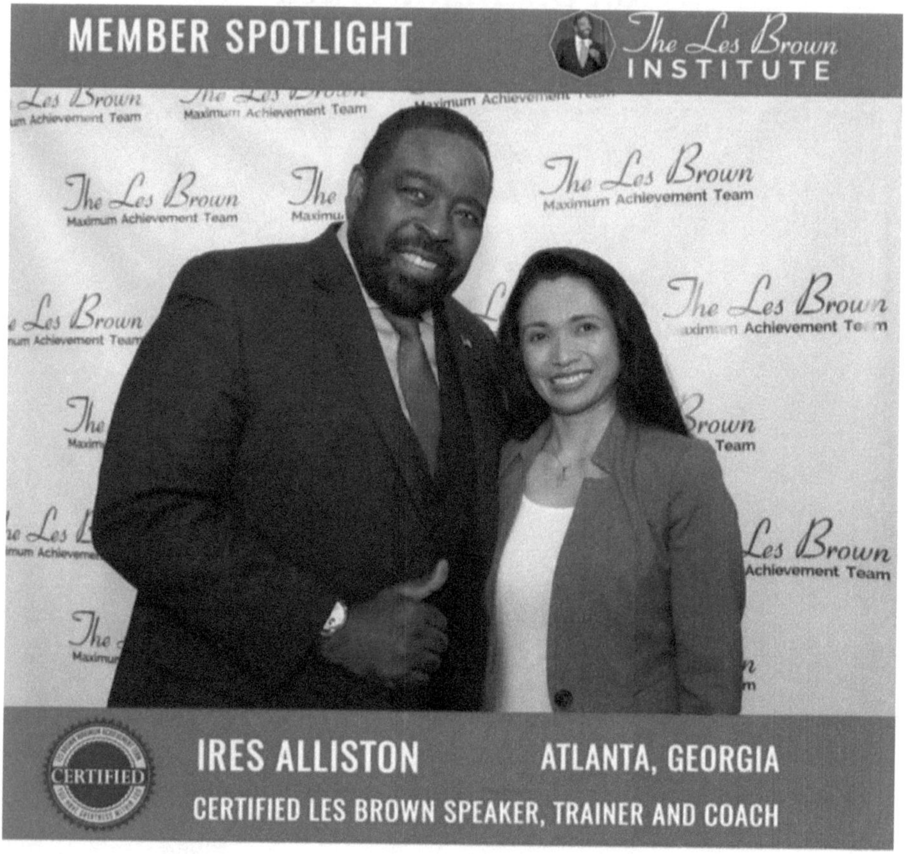

> The best way to get people to *SEE* the value you add to their business is to *SHOW* them the massive *VALUE* you've added to others.
>
> — Ires Alliston

Find something *UNIQUE* that sets you apart from your competition. Become it and speak it to everyone *YOU* meet.

Ires Alliston

Stay *Authentic* and let others see you for who you are!

— Ires Alliston

> *YOU* are your own *HERO!*
>
> Ires Alliston

FOCUS more on what you will do, *NOT* what you won't do.

Ires Alliston

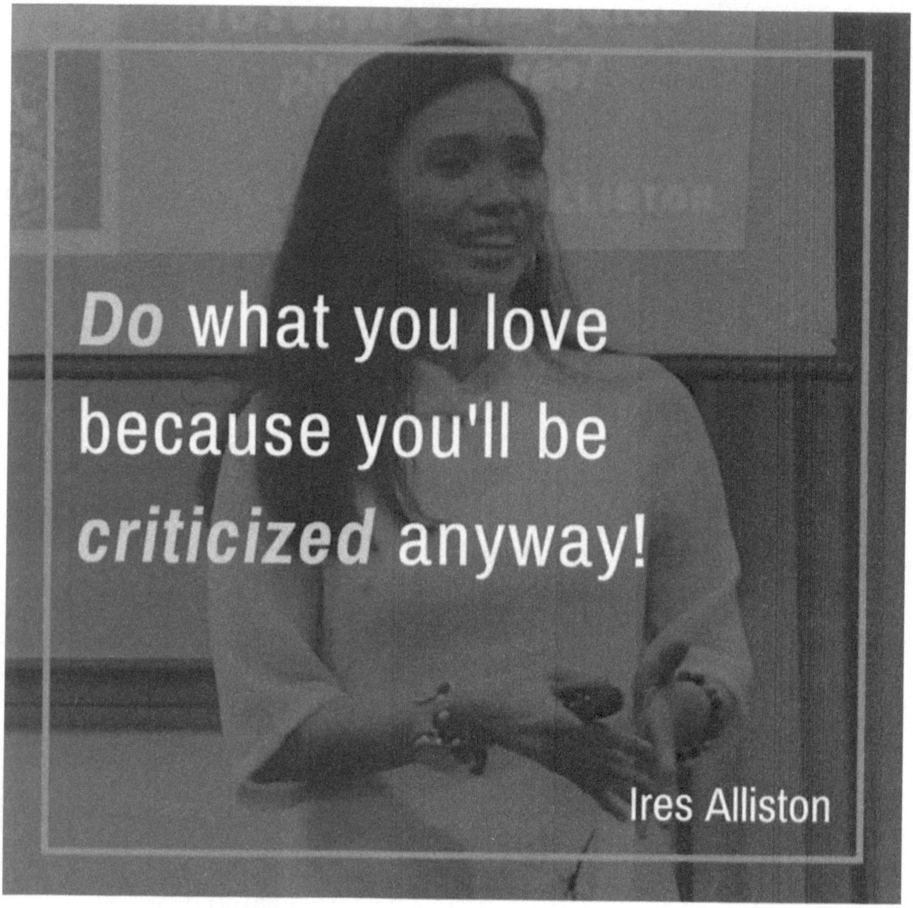

> *Do* what you love because you'll be *criticized* anyway!
>
> — Ires Alliston

If you *find* yourself constantly trying to prove your *worth* to someone, you have already forgotten your *value*.

Ires Alliston

> *Clarity* is the heart of *action*.
>
> Ires Alliston

About Ires Alliston

Being an entrepreneur and founder of the Alliston Group, a digital marketing agency, Ires Alliston helps small business owners and entrepreneurs with branding, marketing, coaching and consulting. With her branding and marketing expertise, Ires certainly has the credentials as a branding expert, marketing mastermind and success strategist. Leadership is also something that comes natural to her, with the ability to lead others to succeed.

She also works with authors, athletes, speakers, trainer, coaches, entrepreneurs and business professionals helping them create trustworthy, credible brands. With her **"Branding for Bosses,"** **"Fast Track Branding Mastery,"** and Strategic Branding and Marketing Blueprint, just to name a few, she creates even more success with her client's business by leveraging the power of their authority in the marketplace, developing their unique selling proposition (or as she calls it, Unique Signature Program), strengthening their digital brand presence and utilizing marketing tools to boosts their brand to another level!

Ires Alliston is an international speaker, trainer and certified coach speaking at events, conferences, summits, and break-out sessions sharing her expertise and knowledge when it comes to business success, branding and marketing.

Media Contact –

Ires is available to keynote, and train corporations, entrepreneurs, and business professionals.

To contact Ires, please either email or call.

Phone: 1-888-978-3258

Personal Website: IresAlliston.com
Email: Info@iresalliston.com
Agency Website: AllistonGroup.com
Email: Info@allistongroup.com

Spark a conversation or follow Ires at any of her social media accounts

Facebook.com/IresDAlliston
Facebook.com/AllistonGroup
Linkedin.com/in/IresAlliston
Instagram.com/IresAlliston
Youtube.com/c/IresAlliston
Vimeo.com/iresalliston
Youtube.com/c/allistongroupllc
Twitter.com/IresAlliston
Twitter.com/AllistonGroup

Recommended Book:
Available at Amazon – Simple Branding Steps for Small Business: It Matters!

Bonus 1:

Bonus 2:

Download the "Branding Checklist" at -
https://allistongroup.com/brandingchecklist

Order on Amazon:
Simple Branding Steps for Small Business: It Matters!

www.ingramcontent.com/pod-product-compliance
Lightning Source LLC
Chambersburg PA
CBHW031535210526
45464CB00003B/1019